Celebrate Your Life!

Readers Rave!

"Using her life philosophy as an example, Melissa empowers those who want to create their own life philosophy. Never dull and always witty, Melissa affirms that life is a banquet to be celebrated every day and provides tips and structure to those who want to learn how to enjoy it."

—Sara Frost, Librarian/Teacher, Wellesley, MA

"This book is indeed about celebrating life. Melissa writes in an engaging, catchy, and up-beat style, concise, witty, an all-round nice read. She provides her readers with a pantry full of organized, interesting tips on enjoying life more fully, ranging from creative fulfillment and personal care to the art of tossing unforgettable parties. It also serves as a fine reminder of highly useful life strategies, things we all know but keep forgetting to put into play. I personally applaud her take on archiving. She suggests some delightful and inventive ways of preserving important mementoes gleaned from family and friends. She also notes the 'enough is enough,' and any archiver must hit the brakes when that 'enough' has been reached, something we all tend to forget."

—Lynn Azzam, Mother/Grandmother/Best Friend, Easton, CT

"Being very visual I was able to apply a lot of Melissa's ideas to lifestyle changes. Her holiday material is useful and enjoyable to read. This isn't about the holidays we all honor (and some of us dread!). It is about making each day an occasion to remember and share. You won't want to miss this wealth of creative ideas to improve your life. Read this book and watch an amazing paradise unfold in your life and home. Thank you, Melissa!"

—Ben Torres, Photographer/Writer, Tucson, AZ

Celebrate Your Life!

"If your celebration of life is on hold, read *Celebrate Your Life!* You will discover the gifts in every day and how you can transform your life from ordinary to extraordinary."
—Lorilee Flynn, Broker Assistant, Atlanta, GA

"One of the many affirmations in this book is, *I take care of my personal image and style by staying up to date,* is very relevant in my life. Too often we are caught surviving by default rather than living by celebration. Much of my work-a-day life circles around textures and colors, and Melissa has brought a lot of ideas to the plate on how to make those textures and colors transfer into your real life. It is a must-have tool for dealing with all kinds of different formats that present themselves in your life."
—Keith McDowell, Hollywood Makeup Artist, Los Angeles, CA

"If you are waiting for an event or circumstance to celebrate, read this book now! Melissa presents a compelling reason to celebrate ourselves, our families, and our friends NOW, each and every day. Don't wait! You may not get that second chance."
—Zuzana Urbanek, Writer/Editor/Consultant, Atlanta, GA

Celebrate Your Life!

The Art of Celebrating Every Day

Melissa Galt

Publishing by Design

Celebrate Your life with Flavor!

Best,
Melissa

Celebrate Your Life!

First printing September 2006

Text design and editing by Zuzana Urbanek, Z-ink.
Cover design by Patricia Rasch.

www.melissagalt.com

Celebrate Your Life!

Dedications

To my mother, the late Academy Award-winning actress Anne Baxter, for leading by example and showing me how to celebrate every day.

To my late godmother, Hollywood costume designer and legend Edith Head, for sharing with me that it is in celebrating others that we truly celebrate ourselves.

To my late great-grandfather, the American architect and icon Frank Lloyd Wright, for inspiring me to share my experiences and philosophies about living a celebrated life and knowing how to celebrate my life's contributions and incredible legacy.

To Filitsa Chigas, my Greek mom and a lady who knows how to celebrate family and friends.

To Lynn Azzam, my Connecticut mom and a dear and wonderful friend, for encouraging me always to celebrate my creative spirit.

Celebrate Your Life!

Table of Contents

Celebrate Your Life!

Celebrate Your Life!

Celebrate Your Life!

Celebrate Your Life!

"The more you praise and celebrate your life, the more there is in life to celebrate."

—Oprah Winfrey

"Celebrate what you want to see more of."

—Tom Peters

"There's a lot happening in many of us. I think you have to celebrate every part. It's what you are. You have to try to find all of those secret names."

—Cassandra Wilson

"I celebrate myself, and sing myself."

—Walt Whitman

Celebrate Your Life!

Don't Wait...Celebrate!

Celebrate Your Life is about just that. It is truly about making each day a celebration. This little book gives you ideas for how you can create special occasions just about any time. It is about transforming ordinary into extraordinary and throwing a party for every reason or no reason at all.

Celebrate Your Life is about renewing and rediscovering our gratitude for each and every day. It is about not waiting for an event or occasion but instead making our own events and occasions because we want to celebrate the goodness of life, the abundance of our blessings, and the great fortune to be alive at this point in time.

Celebrate Your Life is all about you, your family, your friends, and how you can refocus on sharing experiences, developing relationships, and truly connecting in a meaningful way. This is all about reaching out and touching. It isn't about virtuality or cyberspace but entails real-time priorities and magical moments face to face and voice to voice.

Celebrate Your Life is about making life yours and making it special. It is about the wisdom of age, the lessons learned, and avoiding the trap of routine and busy lives to find what matters most and celebrate that regularly. Remember that we each have a choice about how to live. Are you celebrating the choices you are making?

Life moves fast ... if you miss it,
you may not get another chance.
Make this one count and
Celebrate Your Life!

Celebrate Your Creative Spirit

We all have a creative spirit, whether it manifests itself in a talent for home improvement, sewing, craft projects, computer programming, or writing music. Too often we suppress this side as a part of ourselves we will indulge when there is more time. There won't ever be more time, and we need to develop and nurture our creative spirit at *all* times. This will help us to be better balanced and rounded individuals and allows us to share our gifts with others on another level.

Here are some opportunities to celebrate your creative spirit!

Craft Corner

Establish a craft corner or room in your home. This can be as simple as converting the spare/guest room closet into a place for projects that might include sewing, hot gluing, collage making, scrapbooking, and more. It could be as significant as devoting an entire room to these pursuits or creating an exterior work room/tool bench for the pursuit of substantial home improvement projects.

You are more likely to cultivate your creative spirit when you have dedicated space to it and organized the tools and materials needed in an accessible and fun manner.

Celebrate Your Life!

Baskets and boxes of assorted craft materials with a table surface at which to work are often all that is needed. You may even be able to create a makeshift space in a laundry closet by designing a drop-down cover to place over the washer and dryer and using shelving above to store art supplies.

The key is to unleash your creative spirit in a way that works for you. This can also turn into a place for children to work on their school projects.

Celebrate your creative spirit by designing a craft corner or work bench for your creative projects!

Scrapbooks/Scrap pillows

Scrapbooking is now an actual art form. Gone are the days when it merely meant sliding photos between sticky pages and leaving it at that. Today it is about incorporating all manner of mementos with photos and including clever captions, family sayings, and priceless quotes. The challenge is still, of course, to figure out when anyone will slow down long enough to truly enjoy such artistry. I encourage clients to create wall collages instead that can be displayed on stairwells and enjoyed by everyone in the family each day.

Scrap pillows are also a unique idea, and they make great gifts for family. This entails creating a memory pillow with a silkscreen of photos stitched to the pillow and other mementos adhered for a collage effect. This is often most effective in a country or Victorian decorating scheme.

Celebrate your creative spirit by crafting a scrap pillow for a friend or loved one!

Greeting Card Originals

I have a faux finisher and artist friend who makes his own holiday cards. Each is a work of art, and I have to confess that I never opened my birthday card as he had caricatured on the envelope and I didn't want to destroy it! But you don't have to be an artist … start slowly! It may be easier to do this for the occasional birthday than to tackle a major holiday with a host of cards all due. You can use computer imagery, color copies, original photos, and collage items (coins, fabric scraps, charms, trinkets). You can make this a personal statement, and it can even become the gift.

Growing up, I remember that whenever we asked my mom what she wanted, the answer was always the same: a letter from each of us. Yikes, I couldn't buy that and it sounded too easy, so for years I ignored the request and loaded her birthdays and holidays with scarves and picture frames and other goodies. The year I finally listened, she burst into tears because she was so pleased.

Handmade is so rare these days, it means that much more. Tap into your creative spirit to share an original greeting with a friend or family member.

Celebrate Your Life!

Celebrate your creative spirit by putting together greeting card originals!

Recipe Swap

Yes, I can cook—and very well—when I want to, but I hate to follow fancy, complicated recipes and tend to keep my favorites in my head; those with under six ingredients and a limitless variety of add-ins to make it special (or as some friends say, "weird!"). Some of my friends are awesome in the kitchen, turning out dishes that my caterer requests the recipes for! Let's level the field a bit and do a recipe swap. That way we each get some tried and true—and, yes, easy—delicious dishes to share.

Now the fun in this is that you get to sample all the goodies you are getting recipes for. Often this is done at holidays with a cookie swap, but since I am never big on following rules, I do this a couple of times a year and have one for appetizers and another for salads or casseroles. This is not limited to the ladies by any means; many men are great cooks and really enjoy it. Do a kebab recipe swap, a novel idea that gets everybody grilling. Or plan a beverage recipe swap just in time for the heat of summer so you get some fresh punch and summer cooler ideas.

Celebrate your creative spirit in the kitchen with a recipe swap!

Celebrate Your Life!

Garden Magic

I know you think you have a black thumb. Well, get over it. I thought I did too, but only until I really started to dabble in my garden and realized that if something didn't make it, it might not have anything to do with my thumb, but instead with the neighbor's dog, too much sun, or just a finicky plant disposition. Sharing plants and planting tips is a wonderful way to indulge your creative spirit.

Pick a Saturday and plan to spend the time in your garden or a friend's, sharing gardening tips and digging in the dirt. Be sure to have a potted plant or two to say thanks for the help, and these can go in the garden too. (While I love indoor live plants, my pets love them a bit too much as well!) I tend to like an organized chaos of blooms with a layering of color and variety; others are much more orderly and formal in their choices. There is no right or wrong way—you just need to figure out what blooms and what needs extra care.

Celebrate your creative spirit with forays in growing your garden!

Photo Memories

One of the best gifts I ever got was from a friend who had spent Thanksgiving at my home with another friend. She took photos and put them in a small album. They chronicled my oven catching fire from marshmallows in the sweet potatoes (you do know this tradition, don't you?), then the arrival of the fire department, much to my embarrassment. I offered the boys a bottle of champagne for their trouble but they politely declined. She then proceeded to land the same sweet potatoes on her blouse during dinner! It was a riot and the picture album stayed on my desk for over a year, a happy reminder of a wonderful holiday with friends.

The power of photos is often underrated and, while until digitals appeared, I had the unique knack of cutting off people's heads and being perpetually out of focus (thank goodness for digital do-overs), I now take photos everywhere and share them widely. It is a way to capture the present for the future.

Celebrate your creative spirit with digital memory making or just old-fashioned snap shots!

Paint a Plate

Sometimes we can take a lesson from the craft projects kids bring home. I often see painted plates in clients' homes, and I am familiar with the trend of the last few years to go to a do-it-yourself pottery source where you can paint your own plates and have them fired for use at home. This is an easy creative outlet, and it's fun to wrangle friends or family into joining you.

You can either make the plates for decorative purposes or for everyday use. You could even make one as a gift and have everyone sign it with a quote or quip. Personal touches count in a world where we can buy everything.

Celebrate your creative spirit with personal plate opportunities!

Sign a Pillow

I used this idea when I was back in grade school and realize I am going to resurrect it for my next bash. A large canvas style pillow and a package of colorful Sharpie markers can take the place of a guest book and then be tossed into your décor for a memory-making accent. Each person who comes in signs the pillow with a comment about the event, and it becomes a personal reminder of a great time.

If you want to carry this a step further, have everyone sign a flat piece of fabric and when you have collected enough of these from a few years of celebrations, they can be put together to form either a wall tapestry of memories or a floor cloth (sealed with polyurethane). Tap into your creative spirit for preserving moments of celebration.

Celebrate your creative spirit with a pillow or tapestry signing as a decorative memento!

Celebrate Your Life!

Jewelry Making

There is such a wealth of bead-making places available now both at craft shows and in malls. This is another fun way to realize your creative spirit with handmade baubles and bangles. Whether you make something for yourself or family or friends, it is personal and unique.

This won't appeal to all. For example, I'd just be interested in picking the beads out and then moving on and letting someone else do the assembling, but then rumor has it I have ADD! There is still creativity involved, and I have friends that would defer on the bead selection and delightedly sit patiently and string them all. (It is great when opposites attract!)

Celebrate your creative spirit with the making of bright and shiny objects!

Home Improvement

You may be one of those TV wonders that keeps up with all the DIY shows and can actually DIY a project! I admire you and applaud you—I am not. This is a creative gift and can save you a lot of money in labor costs, plus be a rewarding celebration of your own creative spirit.

Whether you want to tackle a dog house complete with lighting and air conditioning (yes, a friend just did this!), or build a deck off the back of the house, or maybe try something on a slightly smaller scale like a simple bird house on a stake, have fun with it. Get the kids involved if you have any and be open to help from friends and family.

It is not about doing it yourself but about sharing your creative spirit with others in a generous manner that really makes the difference.

Celebrate your creative spirit with a home improvement project!

Affirmations

I nurture and encourage my creative spirit by dedicating time for projects I enjoy.

I share my creative spirit with others when I can help them foster their own creativity.

My creative spirit takes many forms and is not limited to what others think is creative but can include my own ideas.

I will grow my creative spirit by my willingness to try creative pursuits that are new to me.

My creative spirit is in all I do, and it is a way to make today a part of tomorrow.

Celebrate Your Life!

Celebrate Your Health and Well-Being*

So often we get caught up in our daily routines only to forget the most important element in our lives: our health and well-being. We are so busy taking care of everyone and everything else that we ignore ourselves until we either get sick or end up at the doctor with an injury. While none of us will ever admit to having the time to be ill or injured, we often don't allow the critical time for health and well-being. When we honor ourselves and our bodies, we will have a greater opportunity to experience the wellness necessary to keep up with and care for our families, enjoy time with our friends, succeed in our work, and make a positive difference to ourselves and others.

*I am not a medical professional and all recommendations here are based on extensive personal experience and that of family and friends. I would encourage you to speak with a trained medical professional regarding your own physical limitations and challenges before following any advice.

Here are some great ways to celebrate your health and fitness.

Celebrate Your Life!

Daily Exercise

Establish a routine that works for you. If you are a morning person and can add in even 30 minutes a day at the front end for a brisk walk, a spin on a bike (stationary or otherwise), yoga stretches, Pilates, or whatever makes you feel good, do it. I literally block my fitness time on my calendar and won't schedule anything over it. It is my time to feel good, get my heart rate up, and break a sweat! So many of us spend much of every day sitting in a car, in an office, on the sofa, at a table—we really do need to make an effort to keep our body active and in tune.

If you are a night owl and prefer to schedule your routine later in the day, make that commitment and create it to work for you. Usually doing exercise right before bed is not wise, as it tends to generate more energy than rest, but perhaps after work or before dinner you can salvage 30 minutes for fitness.

Often we get trapped into thinking that if we can't devote at least an hour, it isn't worth it. This is inaccurate thinking and creates an excuse for not stepping up to take care of ourselves. I have found, as have many others, that a short regular routine that I do faithfully every day energizes me and renews my commitment to myself.

Celebrate your health and well-being with a daily exercise routine!

Celebrate Your Life!

Meditation or Prayer

I like to add this on to my exercise routine, as this is exercise for the mind and heart. While I know you can go to classes on meditation and that most programs demand 20 minutes to over an hour, I find that even 10 minutes at the opening of my day and 10 minutes at the close of my day can give me greater peace of mind and quiet any anxiety or concerns I may have.

This is an invaluable opportunity to clear your mind of all the daily priorities, obligations, and challenges and just tap into that inner quiet place we each have. (Yes, you do have it too!) This may seem almost impossible at first, as few of us are accustomed to sitting completely still for any length of time. We always have something distracting us, whether it is a computer, television, phone, or someone else in the room. This is time free of distractions and interference, time with just yourself.

If you have time, do explore the meditation and prayer classes offered at local centers, churches, and by individual practitioners. You may find your own road to peace of mind that much faster.

Celebrate your health and well-being with a meditation moment!

Celebrate Your Life!

Cleansing

While I do have friends that swear by a regular colon cleanse, this can be time consuming, not always comfortable, and costly. You don't have to go to extremes to get valued results. Cleansing can be as simple as taking one day a week or month to rid your body of the accumulated toxins by drinking at least half your body weight in ounces of purified water only (if you weigh 150 pounds, drink 75 oz. of water, a good daily practice as well)—no soda, no coffee or tea, no juice, no alcohol. Consume nothing more than raw fresh fruits and vegetables.

If you prefer, you can find any number of prescribed cleanses both online, in health food stores, and at your local spa that will allow you the chance to get your body back in balance and give it a break from all the junk we so often consume. This is also a chance to become alcohol- and caffeine-free. Giving up white sugar and flour products can also be very freeing. Many of us have accumulated allergies to foods we eat regularly and just ignore the uncomfortable side effects. A cleanse can allow the body an opportunity to rebalance, providing an increase in energy level, the need for less sleep, and sharper mental clarity.

Celebrate your health and well-being with periodic cleansing!

Healthy Eating

IBS, otherwise known as Irritable Bowel Syndrome, and acid reflux are modern diseases caused by reactions to foods we have been eating for a long time. With our lives often overloaded with stress and anxiety, our bodies now react to what once caused no trouble at all. Rather than taking a lot of pills to conquer the symptoms of these illnesses, it makes more sense to find out the root cause and deal with it directly. Often the medications only mask a larger problem and don't address something as simple as lactose intolerance or an allergy to gluten (yes, this does knock out a lot of foods, but there are just as many that are still available and delicious and won't cause painful side effects).

One of the keys to getting back our balance is to reevaluate our diets and pay more attention. This is not about going on a permanent diet unless you want to. I hate the word diet; it implies limitations and the inability to enjoy what I want. I prefer instead to eat consciously and pay attention to what my body is asking for. Rarely is it screaming for the cookies, muffins, and desserts I think I want or that are fast and easy. Instead it usually wants a balance of protein, carbs, and fats that will leave me with energy and vitality. We all know that when we indulge in a large lunch loaded with carbs, like that Mexican taco special or the pasta buffet, that we are ready for a major nap by mid afternoon. We also know that if we indulge less and instead reach for a salad with chicken or tuna and skip the bread and pasta, we'll be more productive, less forgetful, and stay more on track through the remainder of the day. It is easy to get lazy, but truly the only ones we hurt are ourselves when we don't honor our bodies with healthy eating. Are you listening to your body?

Believe me, I have tried just about every diet on the market at one time or another with very little success, or at least no success that lasted more than a month. From Atkins and South Beach to OPTIFAST and just plain old fasting, I've done the ketosis diet, the cabbage and orange juice cleanse diet, Weight Watchers and more. I've battled weight almost my entire life, but I have found that what works the best is listening to your body and knowing the consequences of ignoring it. Even 10 extra pounds will leave you feeling lethargic, uncomfortable, and uninterested in activities you might usually enjoy. We all make excuses: we are short for our weight, we are fluffy (my favorite!), we are overweight not fat (what is the difference?), we are bloated (every day?), it's hormones, it's PMS, it's our job … It isn't. It is simply that we are out of control and not honoring our bodies and celebrating the health we deserve.

Please know that I am not suggesting that you replace all your favorite foods with organic substitutes, as often you will be dissatisfied with the lack of flavor and cardboard consistency! I know; I have tried this. I have also learned that attempting to find an energy bar that tastes as good as a balanced meal is virtually impossible. These should be used sparingly and as a meal-on-the-go. Too often I've known folks who have substituted energy bars for candy bars or added them to their diet multiple times a day as a snack, not realizing that, while the calories may be better allotted to protein instead of carbs, they are still extra calories that will add up at the end of the day and show up on the scales at the end of the week and month.

Celebrate your health and well-being with healthy eating!

Regular Check-Ups

How often do we make sure that our kids are well cared for by the pediatrician and that our aging parents get to the doctor regularly, but we ignore our own needs for regular check-ups? Our bodies are like cars and need to go in for periodic check-ups and sometimes tune-ups. We are far more likely to avoid significant illness if we stay on top of our health. I am not suggesting going in for every ache or pain, but regular preventive maintenance can be far more time effective and cost efficient than periodic major overhauls and breakdowns.

Women don't enjoy mammograms any more than men look forward to prostate exams, but they are necessary to ensure our continued good health and to head off any possible challenges as early as possible. When you are scheduling the kids and your mom and dad, take time to schedule yourself.

Celebrate your health and well-being with regular check-ups!

Celebrate Your Life!

Happy Smiles

Regular dental care is also a vital part of our overall health. Fortunately, with the advent of tooth whitening, painless dentistry, invisible braces, and other advances, many more people have become aware of the significance of dental health and the relative ease of having a great smile. Teeth cleaning twice a year and x-rays to determine cavities at least once a year are good preventive maintenance steps; they are also often covered by dental insurance and, if not, the price is worth it to avoid much more costly work down the road.

Celebrate your health and well-being with good dental hygiene for happy smiles!

Masterful Massage

Not just for special occasions anymore, massage is often recommended monthly or even weekly to relieve stress, work on overused muscles, and improve relaxation. The key is to find the best massage therapist for you—and they do vary widely, just as there are many different types of massage. Whether your preference is shiatsu, deep tissue, or finger touch, you can do some simple research either through a doctor's office or online and often get a discounted initial session to literally get a feel for each professional's touch.

If this seems too extravagant or you want the ultimate in massage convenience, look into the many massage chairs currently on the market. It is amazing how effective technology can be in delivering a truly refreshing and soothing experience. Many such chairs offer as many as six different types of touch and are engineered to cover your entire back, and some even have built-in leg and foot massage as well.

Massage improves circulation and digestion, in addition to relieving stress and aches and pains. Now you have no excuse not to feel good and get rid of some of that stress we all carry around.

Celebrate your health and well-being with a massage!

Take a Deep Breath

Have you ever been really anxious about something or been moving much too fast, and someone said to you, "slow down and take a deep breath," and you did and it helped? Few of us truly breathe correctly using our diaphragm muscle. Most often we are just doing a quick shallow breathing that keeps us alive but isn't really imparting the benefits of oxygen to our entire bodies. When we focus more on breathing (typically pivotal in meditation), we find ourselves calmer, more centered, and more alert and aware.

This is especially true if we have a chance to get some really fresh air during the course of a day, not easy with constant transitions from car to interior spaces so often polluted with toxic off-gassing materials, airborne germs, and other pollutants. And just going outside is no guarantee, as you know when you hear smog alerts and realize the number of contaminants present in the air around us.

Find your space for clean air, whether it is a few moments outside in the garden, your neighborhood park, or a trip to the botanical gardens. Where you find healthy plants, you find healthy air and can breathe easier.

Celebrate your health and well-being by breathing deeply daily!

Music for Your Ears

When was the last time you had your hearing checked? Why is it that as children we get everything checked regularly and as adults we wait for a problem? Our ears are constantly bombarded by not just vocal noise but musical noise, TV noise, traffic noise, computer noise, children noise, electronic noise, and many other types we aren't even aware of.

Have you ever had the power go out when you didn't think there was any noise? Suddenly you realize how loud quiet really is. When the power goes out, clocks stop ticking, computers stop humming, fluorescent lights stop whining, and so much more that we don't even tune into, but it is there. Our ears are constantly assaulted and it behooves us to have them checked at least every couple of years to ensure continued health and great hearing.

Celebrate your health and well-being with regular hearing check-ups for auditory health!

Windows to Your Soul

Yes, I do mean your eyes, and I'm betting you haven't had them checked lately or if you did it was to get a new prescription! When I was growing up, my sister had what they call a lazy eye. She didn't wear glasses but did do eye exercises daily that strengthened and corrected the condition. She is glasses-free to this day some 30 years later. Unfortunately many of us don't take care of our vision; we read computer screens until we are blind, don't pay attention to proper lighting, and generally abuse that delicate instrument known as our eyes.

It is so much easier to go in for an annual check-up than to wait until it is too late. Many challenges at the early stages can be corrected by exercises or better care. Waiting until later may require drastic measures like LASIK surgery (I know many have experienced great success with this, but any time you can maintain health and avoid surgery is preferred, as there are no guarantees). Glasses are often not necessary at all, and most of us don't want them. (However, sunglasses are increasingly important in this day and age of global warming and the loss of the ozone layer. The glare and UV today takes a serious toll on our vision daily.) Contact lens can be a real

Celebrate Your Life!

hassle. There is no reason to presume that you will need glasses, particularly if no one in your family history wears them (yes, genetics does play a role). Keep the windows to your soul open and without visual aids.

Celebrate the health and well-being of your eyes with regular optical check ups!

Take care of yourself, honor your body and mind, and celebrate health and well-being for life.

Affirmations

I am healthy and honor my body with exercise and fitness every day.

I enjoy the energy I receive from exercise and fitness.

By honoring my health and wellbeing, I honor myself.

Healthy eating provides the essential nutrition and nourishment I need for good health.

Cleansing allows me to rebalance by body and rejuvenate my mind.

Through meditation/prayer I am able to tap into my inner peace and wisdom daily.

Celebrate Your Life!

Celebrate Your Family

I have yet to meet anyone who wishes they spent more time in the office or on their career. Instead everyone seems to miss time with family and friends. Family is not limited in this discussion and context to those related only by blood. Many of us have our truest and best family by virtue of lasting friendships and not blood relations at all. Many of us have very dysfunctional immediate families and it is often not comfortable or enjoyable to share time with them and partake in the dysfunction.

I believe that family is whomever you choose it to be, whether by birth and blood, or by choice and opportunity. It doesn't make sense to sacrifice your precious time off with relentlessly toxic relatives. We all have them, those that just make us crazy on some—or every—level. The ones that believe they are victims in life and are looking for a rescue; the sister that lives in perpetual crisis and with whom any conversation proves exhausting; the deadbeat nephew or niece that just can't get his or her act together and plays woe-is-me as a theme song; or the father that never was one and never wanted to be one.

I don't believe in trying to change these folks or even influence them. I respect their limitations but also know that if being around them is not rewarding, I can make the choice not to be. My life and time here is my own and is too precious to allow the toxic types to rob me of it. I have had the extraordinary privilege of knowing so many people who are so wonderfully gracious to be with and give so much that they are who I choose to share my time with and call family.

It is vital to make a truly conscious effort to celebrate our family often in fun and rewarding ways.

Here are some tried and true and even a few new ideas for celebrating with your chosen family.

Family Dining Delights

Establish a day—and this can be any day of the week—when everyone in the family commits to meeting in one place to share a meal together. It is a weekly opportunity to celebrate each family member's triumphs and support them through their challenges. It is a chance to share advice and give feedback when asked. This can be done at one individual's home or perhaps rotated weekly. It could also be at a favorite restaurant so no one has any setup or cleanup. Often it is a tradition passed down through generations or started by your mother or even mother-in-law. But regardless, if you don't have the tradition, you can create your own.

Celebrate your family with regular dining-out nights!

Celebrate Your Life!

Regular Reunions

Often these are held only every five years or so, with relatives coming in from around the globe to congregate, catch up, and celebrate family time. While reunions can require a great deal of planning and coordinating, it can be fun to do it on a smaller scale annually with those in a specific proximity. We have the large gatherings every five years, but it seems each time there are more folks that I don't know or, goodness forbid, just don't remember. Five years can be a very long time in this age of instant everything.

My aunt does an annual trip with her children and grandchildren for two weeks to some exotic locale. This seems a wonderful way to bring together everyone in her immediate family. Exotic for them means Africa or Australia but to you it could mean Disney World or Detroit. It isn't so much about where you meet but that you do get together and share face time.

We are all so accustomed to electronic means of communication that we forget that face-to-face enables communication on a whole different and more integral level. When face-to-face, we get the gift of expression, vocal intonation, gestures, and body language. We also get the gift of touch that is so often ignored, repressed, or forgotten in the age of virtual relationships.

It seems sad to me that too often today we find ourselves seeing long-lost family only at weddings with all the attendant pomp and circumstance, or at funerals or memorial services with their protocols and guidelines, and there isn't enough time or effort made for family fun connections.

Celebrate your family every day!

Family Ties and Technology

Consider the fun in perhaps selecting a day a month and devoting it to catching up with family. The easy part is, if you put these on the calendar at the beginning of each year, you have this to look forward to. Make this a casual get together.

Now this is where technology can really help. If you can't all get to the same city, agree to a conference call or a family circle call (way less business-like!). As much as I advocate face-to-face, I know that sometimes it just isn't possible. Using technology to facilitate staying in touch makes sense. Why not create a family-exclusive chat room, call it "family talk," and have specific times that everyone jumps on to share news, latest wins, and support in the case of challenges or losses.

Celebrate your family with the help of technology and a family circle call-in!

Family Sport Saturday

Many families have children involved in Saturday sports. What better way to celebrate your family than to extend an invitation to the next game or the playoffs to your extended family. Regardless of win or lose, you can share time catching up in the stands and afterwards with a post-game pizza or other festive fare.

It also seems that too often one parent is designated to attend the games while the other either goes in to the office or takes care of other children. Try to occasionally coordinate efforts so that everyone can be at the same game and cheer on that player, then change it to do the same for the other children later. Include aunts and uncles too, particularly single ones; often we love just that kind of time with our families.

Celebrate your family with a family sporting day!

Botanical Garden Family Outing

Most major cities have botanical gardens and many smaller ones do as well, or at least a wonderful well-planted park, that encourages picnicking with play areas for children or provides an in-depth plant education.

It is funny to me that to this day the education my mother gave us growing up about plants still sticks. Half the time I don't remember how I learned about a certain plant, but I know that it was likely on a nature hike or a botanical garden stroll with Mom. Now, I'm not talking about knowing all the Latin names and roots thereof but just about the delicate beauty of Queen Ann's Lace, the breathtaking aroma of roses in their many varieties, the tender droop of a Lady Slipper, the heady scent of hyacinth, the happy sunshine of daffodils, and the elegance of bearded iris, to name but a few.

Even just learning a little about the myriad evergreens from pine and fir to arbor vitae and the shade-loving hostas and ferns can be a lot of fun for kids. They are too often cooped up inside with their attention captured only by a computer screen and keyboard.

I actually had what I considered to be a black thumb for many years, only to find that when I took an active interest in gardening and did it for fun, I had really good luck with a range of plants and have been able to create a kind of spontaneous jungle of beautiful blooms.

It is easy to include children in the art of planting and then decorating the garden with sculptures, mercury glass, and more. Give each child a small plot to cultivate and call their own, and watch the wonder and joy when they see their plants growing and producing fruits or flowers. If you are in a smaller home without a yard, window box gardens do just as well.

Celebrate your family in the garden!

Blockbuster Movie Family Pack

While you can blow a bundle and take everyone to the movies, complete with popcorn, orange gooey nachos, and gargantuan sodas, you can also do this at home and still provide the popcorn, more moderately sized refreshments, and skip the pseudo-food.

My clients have found that even a large TV in a great room is enough to keep family together and entertained for an evening or a rainy afternoon. If you have the option of doing any size home theatre, there is never a reason to indulge in the high price of movies at the mall. You can even include your own popcorn cart and a mini refrigerator for cold drinks.

Bring Hollywood home and celebrate movies with your family!

Colossal Cultural Family Event

Museums are not always the stuffy places we think they are but often will have exhibits that are family-friendly and sometimes even specific to children. Museums also encompass a scope of venues including natural history (I call these bone museums and they're great favorites for kids) and science museums. I even attended a Garbage Museum not long ago in Milford, Connecticut, devoted to the art of recycling. It was all designed to show our youth the path of goods that get recycled and those that don't. It was fascinating and well done and would make a great family outing.

I remember my mother dragging us (once in a while kicking and screaming) to museums as children, but the lessons sank in and I now go as often as I can and have

31

enjoyed a much broader range of art knowledge because of those trips. It likely influenced even my career decision. Exposing children to art early can have a profound impact on them and, best of all, enjoying art as a family can be a very enlightening experience and provide an opportunity to share a diversity of viewpoints and interpretations of what you view.

Celebrate your family with art and culture!

Six Flags Family Fun Day

Now, it doesn't have to be Six Flags but can be any amusement park including those that offer whitewater fun and rock climbing experiences. The key is to allow everyone a chance to enjoy what each likes and no one is forced to participate but can watch and wait patiently or find his or her own kind of fun.

It often happens that half the family decides to spend time in line for the roller coasters and gravity-defying attractions, while other family members prefer to indulge in face painting, hair braiding, and winning stuffed toys at the toss-it booths scattered throughout. It isn't important that everyone ride the monster coaster but instead that the day starts together, is connected for hair-raising tails of terror and sharing of prizes won, and that everyone heads home happy and tired.

Celebrate your family at a fun park for the day!

Celebrate Your Life!

Family Aquarium Adventure Day

Many major cities now have significant aquariums and often sea water parks if located on the coast. If there isn't one where you live, take a look at which nearby cities (driving distance) offer such attractions and investigate a day trip. These are like ocean zoos and can be great places to learn about the creatures of the deep as well as to share time as a family. Aquariums often include IMAX movies featuring rescue of sunken treasures or stories of underwater predators (movies generally need action and daring-do). In addition they have daily underwater shows with divers portraying mermaids or just interacting with the sea life. This can also be an effective way to encourage swimming and the opportunity to snorkel and scuba.

Celebrate your family with an aquarium adventure day!

Family to Family, a Legacy of Giving

While many of us are familiar with the idea of adopting a child in need, there are also organizations that encourage adoption of a family in need. This may be either overseas or in our own backyard. With such disaster displacement as that of Hurricane Katrina, families were taken in by other families and helped to get back on their feet.

Now, I am not suggesting you necessarily adopt a family into your home, but adopting a family by way of sponsoring them is a great way to start a legacy of giving. So often it is something as little as $30 a month to

Celebrate Your Life!

support a child, so a family might be $100 a month, whereas in our lives that may be the price of a new pair of shoes or a dinner out. This is a chance for everyone in the family to participate in giving and to get to know a family less fortunate.

The added benefit is that it tends to keep us more grounded and aware of our blessings, rather than taking for granted what too few have. Organizations which facilitate this can be found online and through groups such as Habitat for Humanity, The Ruby Slipper Project, Hannah Home, and others.

Celebrate your family by sharing the gift of giving!

Affirmations

I honor time to share with family by choice and by desire.

My family supports me and encourages me in my decisions.

By connecting with family, I enrich my life and share my gifts with those nearest.

I have learned to respect my family members' choices and agree to disagree when best.

I commit to sharing time with my family.

My family makes a positive difference in my life.

Celebrate Your Life!

Celebrate Your Friends

How often do we find that we are losing track of friends without enough time to spend together? It seems easy to say "maybe next month," "when I get that promotion," "when the kids are out of school," or any of a myriad excuses. The bottom line is, if we don't make the time to celebrate our friends, we won't have the time ever. It is all about committing to connect and creating opportunities to make that happen. Be sure to involve everyone in the fun by asking them to bring a dish or other element. No one likes to show up at a party empty-handed, and it is easier if you specify what that is.

Here are just a few ways you can celebrate your friends.

Savory Supper Club

This works well with couples or singles but is usually a kid-free event. This can be a great way to get to know neighbors or other residents in a subdivision. Often its location is rotated monthly between different homes in a neighborhood. A supper club can be very simply created with each couple or person bringing a dish each time; categories are designated to avoid duplicate dishes or too many salads or appetizers. It is a chance for comradery and fellowship, particularly among neighbors.

Celebrate Your Life!

The food preparation duties and expense are shared by all, as are the benefits of original recipes and home cooking. Cleanup is usually light work with many hands, and everyone relaxes and has a good time.

Celebrate your friends and neighbors with a Savory Supper Club!

Super Sporting Event

Make it a real mixed event with singles, couples, and kids, if desired. The sporting event can be live or on TV. If live, plan a festive tailgate to bring everyone together before the game. If televised, set up a buffet for noshing during the game—it can be pot luck, with everyone bringing a dish. Stick with paper plates and plastic cups and flatware for cleanup that's a breeze.

Celebrate your friends with a super sporting event!

Just Girls'/Guys' Night Out

This is Mars's and Venus's chance to have some time to themselves with friends. Often a once-a-month regular event, sometimes once a week, this is a chance to connect with close gal pals or guy buddies and gossip, dish dirt, high five on successes, and commiserate on losses. It can be as easy as establishing a place to meet and a regular date and time and everyone just shows up. Or it can rotate at private homes, but it needs to be understood that it is for just the girls or just the guys.

Celebrate Your Life!

We all share a little differently in mixed company! What is said with this crowd stays with this crowd.

Celebrate your friends with a guys' or girls' night out!

Burning O' the Troubles Bash

Usually I throw this party just after New Year's. It is a great way to get the New Year off to a truly benevolent beginning. Generally this is reserved for adults only. You can make it potluck or provide the food yourself. Each person should bring a listing of their past year's trials, tribulations, losses, and challenges. Using a fireplace or preferably an outdoor fire (a bonfire or chimenea works really well), everyone gets a few minutes alone to literally burn their troubles. Then each guest gets a New Year's party cracker that includes a paper crown which they fill proverbially with hopes for the New Year (some write these on the crown itself) and burn that as a toast to universal energy. I usually end the festivities with sparklers for everyone to have one last sizzle!

Celebrate your friends with a Burning O' Your Troubles Bash!

Oscar Party

The Academy Awards happen in early March, so it is a great chance to catch up and celebrate with friends between New Year's and Memorial Day. It is a dressy function with costumes optional. You can download the ballot forms online, and I encourage ordering party favors and prizes with a Hollywood theme—again, online sources abound. Be sure to start it a little early, before the show begins, so everyone can get comfortable, mingle a bit, and get a bite. Decorate with Oscar statuettes and lots of gold, silver, and black. Go glam!

You'll usually have a handful of die-hard movie fans that will be so intent on watching the awards that they won't really socialize and will shush folks that talk during the show! Having a friend play emcee, if you don't want to do it, can keep the party going with trivia questions and prizes. Everyone wants to win!

Celebrate your friends with an award-winning Oscar night!

Halloween Fright Night

Time to spook it up and get back to the reason Halloween was created. Let's return to scary for just a bit. Come as your favorite ghost, ghoul, monster, witch, or werewolf. This isn't about any stuffed shirt party but a chance to make grunge look good and frightening. You can incorporate trivia here with questions about famous vampires, monsters, and more (sure, Buffy counts!). You may even want to create a mini-haunted house complete with ghostly blow-ups and spider webs and haunting music. Have everyone bring their most terrifying treat to share. Give prizes for the scariest costume!

Celebrate your friends with a Halloween Fright Night!

Broadway Nights

A few girl friends and I got together and bought season tickets to a local community theatre. We go on a Saturday night about once a month and all convene for dinner beforehand at our favorite neighborhood café. It is a lot of fun, and this particular theatre has never let us down with a real variety of plays and great acting talent. I'd like to do the same with a handful of other venues, as it means we have guaranteed seats and a night on the calendar to look forward to.

I have noticed that there are regular groups of couples that get together for the same theatre shows, and even parents with their children who make it a family cultural outing. It is still a celebration of friends!

Celebrate your friends with season tickets to theatre and musical events!

Outlet Therapy

I know that most men don't enjoy shopping (okay, they hate it!) except when it means being left for days at a home improvement center or auto dealership. So to make sure everyone has fun, the guys need to have guy stores to hang out at like Frontgate, Bass Pro Shops, Brookstone, Best Buy, Circuit City, Bose, or any sporting goods store. Usually there is at least one of these in most of the popular outlet shopping centers. Then the ladies can have their occasionally necessary shopping therapy at a discount.

Men are generally quite happy with one or two resources and spending time in research while women enjoy "the more stores the better," flitting from one to the next, always in search of the best bargain (very rarely is it the ideal fit or most flattering look, and many times it will sit in the back of the closet with the tag on, but it will be bragged about as the ultimate steal to fellow bargain hunters!).

If children are in tow, it can be helpful to ensure a stop mid-shopping at a food and entertainment emporium like Chuck E. Cheese's. Savvy retailers often provide play areas to allow Mom better shopping focus. The key is to know that something as proverbially ordinary as shopping can be a chance to celebrate friends, and another pair of eyes is always appreciated to share the virtues of a dress that we might not otherwise need.

Celebrate your friends with a bit of Outlet Therapy!

Goodwill Games (Bunko/Bingo/Bridge/Poker)

I've got a handful of friends that have regularly scheduled game nights separate from a supper club or theatre night. The games are most often played by a group of women or men, rarely mixed, and include bunko, bridge, gin rummy, poker, and even bingo. Crowds range from four to ten plus, and easy eats are provided in the form of sandwiches and appetizers. Jigsaw puzzles could be added to this mix and certainly SCRABBLE, MONOPOLY, Pass the Pigs (really a blast!), and Trivial Pursuit.

This is a really nice change from the monotony and soloness of computer games. It is a good social opportunity and allows for some of the competitiveness to come into play—just no sore losers please!

Celebrate your friends by creating a Goodwill Games night!

Art for the Ears

Recently I attended a concert with friends at Atlanta's Botanical Gardens. It was a beautiful night and, though they were very restrictive in not allowing food or drink brought in, the gardens did provide delicious gourmet fare, beer, and wine by the glass or bottle for purchase. It made it very easy and the venue was smaller and more intimate than a large concert hall or performing arts center. I realized that it wasn't truly important to me who was playing but that it was the comradery and the minimal planning we enjoyed, since we could buy our feast on site only.

Celebrate Your Life!

Whether you are game for an outdoor venue and take your chances with weather or prefer the safety of a music center or playhouse is up to you. Music truly is art for your ears, and it is another fun way to celebrate friends by creating a regular concert schedule to enjoy together. It can include food and beverages picnic style or just grabbing a bite before or after at a local tavern. The point is to share the experience.

Celebrate your friends with time for a concert or other musical event together!

Celebrating time with our friends is one of the best parts of our life experience. It is up to each of us to create that time and make the commitment to honor those relationships.

Affirmations

I am blessed with great friendships because I am a great friend.

I honor my friends by committing to spend time together.

I celebrate my friends often with planned and spontaneous activities.

My friends enrich my life with their diversity and uniqueness.

Friends are part of the essential fabric of my life, and I am grateful always to have them.

Celebrate Your Life!

Celebrate Your Career

More than a third of our lives are spent in pursuit of our livelihood. Too often this is not a celebration but instead an obligation and a decision by default. We are put on a career track before we even know what we truly want to pursue, and by the time we figure it out we have already achieved a level of success and financial reward from which starting anew would mean setbacks and sacrifice. Unfortunately, without the willingness to take risks and sometimes take a new path, we wind up living our work life by default rather than by our own design.

Regardless of where you find yourself in your career, there are ways that you can celebrate that commitment and benefit from your unique skills and abilities (even if your genuine talent rests on another path).

Here are just a few ways to celebrate your career.

Strategic Alliances

I have found that, as an independent business owner, my business appears much larger and stronger with the strategic alliances I have formed with fellow businesses. The same applies to any corporation that aligns itself with other organizations to create a masterful synergy.

Celebrate Your Life!

As an individual, no matter where you work, you can create strategic alliances that will grow your own career. These can be fellow business people whose business goals complement yours and you regularly work together. It can even be a competitor with whom you are able to mutually appreciate the idea that there is enough pie to go around and the more you work together, the greater the share each of you gets.

Take a look around you, both within the organization you work for or have created and outside of it, to identify your strategic alliance partners. Usually it is an informal agreement, though at times you both may benefit from a more structured format with scheduled meetings and planned outcomes.

Celebrate your career by forming successful strategic alliances!

Give to Receive

The old adage "what goes around, comes around" is all too true, and so it is that by giving of ourselves, our expertise, our talents, and our abilities that we truly become rich and will receive the bounty of others. Establish charitable goals for your business, your department, or your position. Make your contributions distinctive and measurable, though it is likely their value will be infinite. Focus on giving and you will be surprised at the gifts that will return to you. Too often we can get caught up in looking for the return. When we give, rarely do those returns show up as we might expect but turn out to be bigger and better than we imagined.

Celebrate your career by giving back!

Mentoring

Not everyone can be an effective mentor, but it is an invaluable gift to others when you can. I have sponsored many an intern over the last decade plus, and I find it incredibly rewarding to be able to show them a true view of my career path and help them see what parts they excel in, where they need further study, and what path they might decide to pursue.

Mentoring can be formal or informal in structure. It can mean a monthly lunch, a phone call twice a year, daily interaction such as with an intern, or a one-time meeting of minds to share hopes and dreams, experiences, and lessons learned. Mentoring is as much about teaching as it is about learning from those coming up.

Celebrate your career by being a mentor!

Lifelines

While we all know the term networking, with many of us being very good at it and others not so hot, it is not about networking so much as about creating networks to live and lifelines for netliving. Networking is all too often that lopsided sort of one-way search for the next big contact; it is looking for who can connect us best rather than the reciprocal idea of netliving, which extends far beyond the workplace to all of life.

Netliving and forming lifelines means cultivating the practice of connecting with many more people than just those at events and in business. It is about spreading the word when you enjoy someone's product or service and you aren't even aware of how your word of mouth will connect them. It is finding out about our dry cleaner, our pharmacist, our dentist and doctor (my doctor actually keeps an eye on the newspaper for clippings profiling or relating to his patients), our favorite restaurant host, the salesperson at our favorite clothing boutique, and the retailer we use most for gifts.

While multilevel marketing is now renamed network marketing, it still may have a negative ring for you, but the lessons it teaches are valuable. Start by creating your network with those closest to home.

Sometimes those we seek most are right in front of us and we just don't think it can be that easy. Don't make it hard…explore the obvious.

Celebrate your career by forming lifelines, not mere networks!

Celebrate Your Life!

Lunch with the Bunch

Both for business owners too busy in their own fields to connect with others and for those in corporate America who feel pigeon-holed in their own specialties, mix it up. That is, make a point once a month to lunch with others outside of your expertise. For business owners this means connecting in a meaningful way with entrepreneurs in other fields. It can create new perspectives and allow us to see new ways to do old things. As a member of corporate America, take a look at what other areas of expertise your company offers and connect with some of those individuals. It will give you a broader understanding of what your company brings to the table as well as provide opportunities to explore innovative synergies amongst diverse divisions.

So often we are too close to the trees to see the forest. Broadening our circle of influence is a successful way to expand our own potential and affiliations.

Celebrate your career by branching out; share lunch with someone not in your field of expertise or not in your business!

Supplier Thank You's

Do you regularly say thank you to those that supply your business? In a corporate setting, do you know what your company does to say thank you to vendors? No business can survive in a vacuum, and while we all are suppliers to someone else, we often forget that we are kept afloat and our success depends on those that supply us. I often send or deliver boxes of Godiva chocolates to my vendors as random thank you's. I don't wait for the holidays, as we all are inundated then—after all, that is the season for thank you. What about the rest of the year? When the ladies at my drapery workroom are really slammed, I'll send in pizza for lunch and, at least twice a year, I send flowers for no reason at all, just to brighten their offices.

Think about your printer, your computer tech, your advertising executive, the cleaning service, the phone repairman, the security system expert. When was the last time you *showed* them "thank you," not just said it?

Celebrate your career by being gracious with others!

Women/Men on the Move

There are many opportunities to grow your mind and your career if you pay attention and make the time. There are roundtables of which you can become an active member and groups for both men and women dedicated to grooming top executives or cultivating entrepreneurship. These are great chances to connect with others beyond your field and learn about their expertise to find potential synergies. It is a question of whether you are ready to lead the same life every day or create a new and unique experience daily. All of life is about growing, and it is only when we stop growing that we truly start to die. Pushing our boundaries, challenging our limitations, and growing our potential can give us a present beyond our dreams and a future without limits.

Celebrate your career by pushing your boundaries and expanding your limitations. Be a Man or Woman on the Move!

Continuing Brilliance

Many of us have a requirement for continuing education built into our careers with necessary certifications or levels of achievement. Even without this, it is essential that we stay on top of the latest developments with classes offered by professional industry organizations, trade shows, special presentations, and more. We often do this early on in our careers but then get caught up in our success and progress and forget to continue our brilliance. We leave these opportunities on the table for those in the early stages of their careers and, in doing so, run the risk of becoming the dinosaurs we read about.

Technology can make learning more accessible and convenient, but it can't replace the synergy of a live group. Often, more is gained through discussion and listening to other queries than from the actual lecture itself.

Celebrate your career by expanding your mind and maintaining your edge!

Celebrate Your Life!

Conferences to Connect

Anyone who has been to a trade show knows that trade shows and conventions are a lot of work. I don't mean just for those who do the planning but also for the attendees. There are always tough choices to make between sessions to attend and then there is all the connecting you want to take advantage of.

I often find that the true experts—those presenting—are most accessible at these events. It seems everyone else thinks they will be unapproachable, so they don't even try, leaving a wide open entrance for me to share in their experiences. Try this next time you attend an event: single out one or two of the presenters you'd like a minute with and try to connect. Sometimes you can wrangle an hour of their time consulting or snag a seat next to them at lunch or dinner and glean a tidbit or two that can transform your journey from the on-ramp to the fast lane.

Be brave and take a chance. Too often we are intimidated (even if we won't admit it) by someone else's perceived success and stature. There will always be those greater than us and those lesser than us; it is up to each of us to determine where we will stand.

Celebrate your career and take advantage of the opportunities for continued brilliance!

Celebrate Your Life!

Share the Wealth

Be generous with your time, your expertise, and your rewards. When I taught "Interior Design as a Second Career" at Evening at Emory for over a decade, I was always amazed when my students—busy professionals exploring the interior design field—told me that I was the first professional to freely share with them the inside scoop including salaries, hours, and the nitty gritty. In fact, my favorite compliment came from a gal who came up to me after class and thanked me for showing her that design was not for her, but she had decided what was, and was thrilled to have made the decision to pursue it.

You see, my job wasn't to convince or sell anyone but just to share my knowledge and experience wholly and completely so any person listening could make up his or her own mind. There are others who felt empowered and encouraged by what I described and have decided to pursue it.

By simply being ourselves and contributing our personal experiences and wealth of talent to others, we can make a world of difference.

Celebrate your career by sharing your knowledge and experience!

Affirmations

I am committed to my career growth and success.

I honor my business associates by sharing with them my time and expertise.

I enjoy continual learning to expand my horizons and maintain my knowledge.

Trade shows and conferences are an essential part of my career success.

Connecting with others both inside and outside of my industry is a valued way of creating opportunities and synergies with and for others.

Celebrate Your Personal Image and Style

Beauty Sleep

One of the hotels I stayed in recently had a really neat bedside kit. It included quilted eye shades to block out the light, a refreshing face tonic to spritz on before retiring, and a short poem about a good night's rest. The hotel also offered the Sleep Number bed and I spent a while tinkering to find my perfect number! Not too hard, not too soft… you know the drill. I realized that too many of us don't pay much attention to what we sleep on, and that means we probably aren't getting nearly the real rest we need.

So many of my clients tackle their bedrooms last and that often means 2 to 3 years down the road from when they started on the great room. And yet we all spend a third of our lives in the bedroom if not always in bed. A good night's rest is essential to staying productive, being energized, and feeling good. The funny thing is, it doesn't have to be anything special like the Sleep Number bed, unless that is your bag.

Many hotel chains have taken to selling their own privately labeled and licensed lines of beds and linens,

Celebrate Your Life!

Westin and The Ritz-Carlton among them. Personally, I've found that the Original Mattress Factory does an excellent job with very reasonable pricing and good service. I also know that you really do have to try out a bed before buying and know that if you don't like it in the showroom, it won't improve at home.

Sheets count too, and many of us grew up with scratchy percale. Now it is commonplace to enjoy 330-count Egyptian cotton available through all major bed and bath retailers and even the mainline discount chains. Make it comfortable, selecting a soothing color palette, and make it inviting after a long day.

Essential parts to every bed—beyond the frame, mattress, box spring, and headboard—are a mattress cover, 2 sets of sheets, 2 sleeping pillows, 2 sham pillows, 1 Euro Sham (the big square one) and a toss pillow or two. Some enjoy many more pillows, others can barely stand one. Make it yours and make it a place you can really rejuvenate each night. Don't forget generously-sized lamps for reading in bed and good nightstands to hold the alarm clock or music for drifting off.

Celebrate your personal image by getting the best sleep possible!

Celebrate Your Life!

Makeover

This is now available for men as well as women, though so far, I am not aware of a men's cosmetic line, only skin care which is vital. It is always fun to find out about the hottest and latest products on the market and give them a try. Certainly many major department stores offer makeovers, and roping in a couple of friends works well too.

If you want a more private treatment consider calling a representative with Avon, Merle Norman, or Mary Kay for a house call. Yes, you likely will need to have a group in to make it worth their while. Of course they expect to sell product, as do the department stores, but there is no obligation and if you love the new look, you can indulge. Don't feel pressured to buy and be sure to check your current stock of beauty supplies first.

Celebrate your personal image and style with a skin care and/or cosmetic makeover!

Wardrobe Redo

Personal shoppers often come complimentary at the larger department stores and, if you find the right one, can do wonders for your wardrobe. Now, this isn't "What Not to Wear," so you aren't bringing in your wardrobe in garbage bags and going through it all, but you can bring selected pieces or pictures of your favorite outfits and find ways to remix, rematch, and add fashionable new accents.

Celebrate Your Life!

Alternatively, you can find custom personal shoppers available locally by searching online or asking some of the boutique stores. These specialists are glad to come out to your home, evaluate your wardrobe needs and then shop for you. Typically they'll bring it back for you to try on, saving you the sometimes agonizing time to shop and select. This works well for men and women alike. I have actually worked with a handful of select clients as a personal shopper with great success. Sometimes alterations need to be made, but this is a valuable chance to find the clothing designers and makers that work best for your shape and style.

Celebrate your personal image and style with a personal shopper to guide you!

Goodwill Weekend

Have you ever followed the rule that for every new thing you purchase, two old things have to go? I bet not, so now your closet is jammed to the gills and you don't even know what you have. What better time than this for a Goodwill Weekend. Invite a handful of close friends over, open up some refreshments, and let the fun begin. Friends can be more ruthless than you might about what to let go. While the guideline is that if you haven't worn it in two years, cut it loose, I find that may not be so easy particularly if it still has a tag and looks great when you are a mere five pounds lighter!

Celebrate Your Life!

You'll also likely struggle with some bargains you found that seemed essential at the time, but the most necessary part was the incredible deal you got. There are lots of deserving folks that would love your hand-me-downs at Goodwill, Salvation Army, Hannah House, and Dress for Success (business wear).

While I agree that all fashion and interior styles come back every 20 years or so, it is not a reason to hang onto your college favorites. You not only have outgrown them (let's get honest!) but the styles just won't look the same the second time around. Some reruns aren't meant to be.

Celebrate your personal image and style with an update and a Goodwill Weekend!

In-Home Shopping

Those of us with too little time or who just hate to shop for clothes will love the in-home shopping opportunities. Several companies offer them including The Worth Collection, Ltd., Weekenders, and CAbi, to name a few. Typically they require that you throw an in-home get-together for a number of friends and associates so that they can show the line to a larger audience. It is still a good deal, and typically the hostess gets discounts off pieces she wants.

The second option is to hire a personal tailor, popular for busy male executives but not as common for professional women. Usually a tailor only handles men or women, not both. While the fabrics used may be similar, the cut and fit are entirely different. This option is generally all about convenience and quality. Be sure to evaluate more than one service to ensure your best fit.

Celebrate your personal image and style with the convenience of in-home clothing purchases or a personal tailor!

Fashion Show

I seem to get notices frequently for these from the department stores where I have shopped. Make it an event with a couple of friends and enjoy the opportunity to check out the latest fashion trends and snappy ways to update your wardrobe. Depending on the level of designer being showcased, the prices may be one-of-a-kind or mass market, but in any case you'll get a good idea of what is hitting the market and whether you want to incorporate it into your wardrobe and personal style. These events often benefit a charitable cause as well, so in addition to expanding your fashion sense, you are giving.

Guys may want to pass on this unless there is a share of the show devoted to men's couture or the models are worth a look. At least if he does go, he'll understand a little more about the latest styles and why you have to have them!

Celebrate your personal image and style by attending a fashion show!

Celebrate Your Life!

Pampered Hands and Feet

No longer just for women, men are learning to indulge in proper and regular care for their hands and feet with manicures and pedicures. While for many this still signifies a special occasion, when you consider that we display our hands every day and in the summer months are usually in open-toed sandals or flip flops, keeping up with hand and foot health and aesthetics makes a lot of sense.

There is a nail salon on just about every corner in most major cities. Find one that works for you. With options like diamond nails, solar nails, acrylic wraps, and more, you'll want to find what works for you. Guys generally just want a great manicure, though some gentlemen opt for clear polish. Be aware that you may be allergic to certain chemicals used. And, if you are only allowing yourself this luxury occasionally, you'll want to get to a spa and squeeze in another treatment.

My favorite idea is to have the manicurist and or pedicurist to my home to give mini treatments to friends at a spa party. With this option, there's no need to worry about putting on shoes too soon after a pedicure … enjoy going barefoot in familiar surroundings.

Celebrate your personal image and style with a regular manicure and/or pedicure!

Celebrate Your Life!

Facial Fun

Again, no longer just the domain of the ladies, men and women alike are enjoying the benefits of facials. It can be a wonderful chance to truly pamper your skin and detoxify from all of the airborne irritants we face daily and the plucking, tweezing, and shaving we torture our faces with.

Facial technicians are known as aestheticians (or estheticians) and are typically versed in a wide range of treatment styles and products. Be sure to read any brochure or online information before signing up to get what sounds like a good fit. Ask questions when in doubt. It is not always as relaxing as you anticipate. Many treatments include removals of blackheads and other skin impurities, and this can be particularly painful for many people. Awareness is the best way to be prepared.

You can certainly put together your own facial at home using steaming face clothes, a cleansing scrub, a toner, moisturizers, and a mask or peel. It is infinitely more relaxing to have someone else in charge.

Celebrate your personal image and style by taking extra good care of your face, your calling card to the world!

Celebrate Your Life!

Spa Afternoon

Or maybe a spa week ... I can't sit still that long, but most of my friends would love that chance! You can do this locally for an afternoon of rest and relaxation or you can opt for a weekend away or even a week in an exotic locale. Be certain to sign up for your treatments in advance as many popular ones will be unavailable at the last minute. This is a great time to try something new like a couple's massage, a hot rocks massage, a vichy shower, a mud bath, or a body wrap. You may not like it all, but you'll have some fun stories to share about the experience and generally you will return looking and feeling more relaxed, energized, and calm.

When you take time for yourself you will be rewarded with greater health and vitality and a refreshed perspective.

Celebrate your personal image and style with a spa retreat long or short!

Signature Style

Do you have a signature style? Do you have a look? How about a piece of jewelry you wear consistently? Style is often about creating a signature. We all know a "hat lady" or the "bowtie guy." Their signature is a unique accessory they typically own many of and coordinate with each outfit. It makes them easy to remember and to spot in a crowd. Perhaps yours isn't just one item but the way you dress overall. Some of us just manage to blend

Celebrate Your Life!

in, often dressing in the dark and still looking presentable. This isn't necessarily a good thing as it indicates a significant lack of personal style.

Style is something that some people are lucky enough to be born with, while others have to learn it along the way and imitate what they see in magazines to make it work. It doesn't matter how you get it, but it is important to get it. We only get a very brief shot at a first impression and our style speaks volumes. What is yours saying?

If you want to create a signature style but aren't sure how, this is the perfect time to enlist the help of a professional shopper and canvas your friends to see if there is something you already wear that stands out. It may take a bit of work, but it will be worth it.

Celebrate your personal image and style by developing a personal signature look!

Affirmations

I honor my personal image by taking care
of my physical appearance.

I always put my best foot forward with
personal style.

I take care of my personal image and style
by staying up to date.

Just as a person's shoes and handbag/wallet
speak of his or her grooming, so do hands
and feet when exposed. I take extra care to
always appear well groomed.

I am developing a personal style that will be
comfortable and unique to me.

Celebrate Your Life!

Celebrate Your Travel and Adventure

With the world growing ever smaller, many of us travel often for business and pleasure. This can be a wonderful and valued opportunity to experience and share in other cultures and customs and learn about others' beliefs. Certainly with all the home goods that we now buy from other countries, it is a chance to truly create lives of global influence and reach beyond our own backyard to enrich our environments and experiences with the world around us.

Here are some distinctive ways to celebrate your spirit of travel and adventure.

Blended Traditions

Whenever I share holidays with friends and their families, I always find new traditions to experience and often enjoy adding one or two to my own. In order to blend traditions, we need to get outside our comfort zone and explore some other customs. Whether it is as simple as adding a new dish to the Thanksgiving feast, or celebrating the New Year with holiday poppers and a

Celebrate Your Life!

Burning O' the Troubles Bash, the point is to open ourselves to new ideas and opportunities.

Until I moved to the South years ago, I had never had (or even heard of) creamed corn or green bean casserole. I was born and raised on the West Coast, home to *nouvelle cuisine* (no casseroles and no sauces), sushi, and granola (before it was a cereal!). Biscuits were something we had from Kentucky Fried Chicken, not ever for breakfast with gravy. Just going from coast to coast or from the North to the South can mean some big shifts in traditions and practices.

Imagine at each holiday if you adopted a tradition from your family's original homeland. Unless you are Native American, you aren't native to the United States and, with the popularity of genealogy today, can trace your roots back generations to those that brought you here. While you may be as close as only a first or second generation and your native traditions are very much intact, many of us have gotten far from our ancestral legacy—this is a valued chance to get back in touch.

Celebrate your travel and adventure by blending traditions!

Sharing Cultures

With our tapestry of friends and far-flung family these days, consider creating a culture exchange evening or weekend with family and/or friends from another country. It is always fascinating to learn about their foods, traditions, dress, and daily routines. We tend to lead very myopic lives, and this gives us a broader view beyond our comfort zone.

Learning about another family and how they live can make us more compassionate and expand our understanding of environmental influences, historical differences, and unique customs.

There are also valuable opportunities to do this with organizations devoted to particular ethnic groups. The larger metropolises often have a French Alliance, a German Exchange Club, a Korean Center, and such. These organizations usually put on a cultural exchange a couple of times a year, inviting outsiders in to partake of the special customs, products, and foods of their countries. Check these out to expand your understanding without ever leaving the city! Enjoy a taste of the unknown right here at home.

Celebrate your travel and adventure by sharing cultures!

Mementos to Cherish

This is all about knowing what to collect when traveling, and I don't include the plastic key chains found in airport gift stores or the decorative refrigerator magnets (though they can be fun to collect!). Before you head out the door, do just a minimal amount of research about your destination. Find out what the country is best known for. In Italy it is the leather goods, in Ireland it is crystal, in Vermont it is the maple syrup and maple sugar products, in Africa it is native masks. Each destination, whether domestic or international, has a specialty and it is most memorable and fun if you can bring back a unique sample of that locale.

An alternative is to collect the same memento from each country. For example, I have often picked up wonderful original roadside watercolors when traveling, whether it was in Greece, Nepal, or New Orleans. Each is markedly different in its depiction of native landmarks and towns, but they have the common thread of watercolor as their medium.

These pieces can serve as valued memory guides to the stories of the trip you took. They are markers of the time spent and adventure experienced. These are also quite personal, as in many cases you have the chance to meet the artist or artisan that crafted the piece.

Celebrate your travel and adventure with cherished mementos!

Stories to Tell

Be sure to keep a travel journal with you for all the stories you collect. Some will be wild and wacky, others fascinating and filled with intrigue, and others even a bit daring (like bungee jumping). It is stories that our lives are truly made up of, and so often we are caught up in the moment only to find our memory weeks later is not as reliable as we supposed. At the end of each day or beginning of the next, just jot down some of the highlights and certainly any critical names of places visited and people you connected with. This can also be a great addendum to any photo album you create, serving as a written roadmap of adventures shared.

Celebrate your travel and adventure by journaling your stories to tell!

Dress the Part

I am always fascinated by the costume of foreign cultures, whether it is lederhosen and frock dresses in Switzerland or brilliant silk saris in India. Often our fashion is influenced by all manner of international clothing. It may be fun to make it a point to pick up a certain piece of clothing from countries visited; something as simple and easy as a scarf to wear with coats and jackets would be a handsome reminder of the trips you've taken and a practical element to add to your wardrobe. Hats are another fun idea that can be taken from virtually any culture.

Now if you aren't really interested in fashion, at the least you can collect ball caps from other locales (yes, likely available in the airport gift shop!). These can be emblazoned with local flags, colors, coats of arms, shields, or other motifs indicative of that state or country.

Celebrate Your Life!

Celebrate your travel and adventure by learning the mode of dress and fashion in other countries!

A World Away Party

One of the best parts of any trip is, once you have gotten home and back in your routine, to plan a "world away" party to share with family and friends your experiences abroad (or just out of state!). Encourage everyone to bring a dish from that culture. For example, Italy is easy with pasta and pizza, New Orleans is Cajun and blackened, the South is mashed potatoes and fried chicken, England is steak and kidney pie and mincemeat pockets.

You can plan a presentation of your photographs, no longer just slides, but PowerPoint-ed! Perhaps you took a video camera and have some entertaining video to share. You can also run this in the background of the party repeatedly to just give the flavor of your travels (sometimes trips aren't as fascinating to those who didn't go).

Encourage guests to dress the part with something they associate with that country or area. This is a fun way to rekindle the spirit of travel and transport everyone to that place for even just a few hours.

Celebrate your travel and adventure with a World Away Party!

Celebrate Your Life!

Tribute to Travels

While certainly you can create a wonderful visual presentation about your travels to share with friends and family, this is more about celebrating your experience on a daily basis. I always feel transported to another world when I walk in my front door and see my Indian tapestry hanging over the living room daybed, and glimpse the masks I brought back from Africa gracing one wall.

Celebrate your travels with the mood from afar right here at home. More than a global influence or a tradition, it is about connecting with the world through our experiences, the stories we've collected and shared, and how we live with these each and every day. Many of my clients have homes that bespeak international adventure (and business), and this also reinforces their global spirit and their compassion for other cultures. Collecting personalizes their lives and creates a portal for mind travel at any moment.

Celebrate your travel and adventure by creating a tribute to your travels right here at home!

Influences from Afar

I grew up in a home that was laden with global influences. We had Persian rugs on the floor, a Flokati rug from Greece in the living room, a Chinese opium bed as a sofa, and a bar transformed from a Mexican chest. It was a great lesson in international culture and influenced my love of travel and my design sensibilities.

Celebrate Your Life!

Many of us today have many international influences in our homes just by virtue of shopping at places like Pier 1 and Cost Plus World Market. Typically, labor overseas is much less expensive than here at home, so imports abound. Think even just in terms of elements like pillows, lamps, candleholders, and a decorative box or basket. Whether it is Indonesian, Asian, African, South American, or from South Carolina (incredible pine needle baskets and sweet grass woven goods), it adds a layer of character and interest not possible if you keep it all homogenous from one country and culture.

The United States is truly a melting pot, so take advantage of the rich cultural mix we have around us and enliven your home and life with a more global flavor.

Celebrate your travel and adventure by showcasing influences from afar in your home!

Distant Connections

Stay in touch with those you meet abroad. Often we are more open when traveling and truly meet some interesting characters. By the same token, too often we forget to get their contact information, or if we do get it, when we return we are so busy getting caught up with our regular commitments that we forget to stay in touch.

Celebrate Your Life!

In this day and age of instant communication, it is easy to transcend the barriers of time zones and unreliable snail mail. You can use email, text messaging, telegram, fax, or even old fashioned (and always welcome) letters to keep in touch.

The flip side of this is to stay in touch with family and friends when you are traveling. I often send postcards to all of my clients and friends when out of state. I print off mailing labels before I head out to make this easy and then just make a point of getting local postage once I arrive at my destination. You don't have to write a lot but let them know you are thinking of them and add to their file of places to visit.

Celebrate your travel and adventure by mastering the art of staying in touch with distant connections!

Language Lessons

While English is the most used language in the world today, it is important that if we truly want to experience another country, we consider indulging in lessons of their language. We may not become fluent or proficient, but the fact that we are trying with just a few simple phrases and an accent does make a difference.

I've found that foreigners are much friendlier when they see me making a genuine effort rather than being the typical American tourist that expects it all in our native tongue, not theirs. Besides, we are foreigners to them when we are visiting their country!

Celebrate your travel and adventure by learning a foreign language!

Affirmations

My travels allow me to fill my life with global influence.

I am fascinated and intrigued by other cultures and customs.

My life is richer for the privilege of travel and adventure.

I expand my boundaries and limitations with every trip I take.

I promote my compassion and understanding for all of humanity through travel and adventure.

Celebrate Your Life!

Celebrate Your Home

Home is truly our external heart and, as such, it needs a lot of care and attention in its decorating and development. Invite friends and family to contribute to the creation of your home. A house is merely a dwelling … it becomes a home when you use your heart to express yourself in a comfortable and inviting manner.

Here are some easy ways to celebrate your home with friends and family.

Housewarming by the Room

So few people remember to throw a housewarming or, if they do, it is a couple of years after moving in. So, to get this ball rolling, don't wait for the entire house to be complete; instead, celebrate room by room. Very few folks decorate their entire home at once anyway, and it counts to measure the small successes, even if it is a powder room, not to mention the big successes like a kitchen or bath remodel.

How many entertaining opportunities have you missed by waiting to get your house complete? Remember, if your friends are waiting to see your drapery and not you, you might want to consider some new friends! Life is in

Celebrate Your Life!

the connection, not in the stuff. Celebrate every step rather than waiting for just one big one.

Celebrate your home with room-by-room housewarmings!

Stock the Pantry Party

No one likes to show up at a party empty-handed and this is an easy way to get guests to bring what you need and want, while you share the warmth of your home and hospitality.

Create a master list of pantry stockers desired or even register if you are including kitchen appliances like blenders, toasters, and food processors. Let everyone know what you are into, whether it is a pantry full of bottled water and chips and dip, or you are a bit more of a cook and want great exotic spices, tins of imported specialty foods, and international flavors. Sure, flour and sugar are necessary staples, but I bet you can get more creative.

When it comes to appliances and kitchen tools, think hard about what you want and what you'll use. Of course, some are still almost required like the blender and toaster, but what about a divine bread maker, the latest ergonomic palm-held peeler, a butterfly trash can by Simply Human, or a classic wine rack. You can even suggest gift cards from favorite big box retail kitchen goods stores like Bed Bath & Beyond, Williams-Sonoma, and Crate&Barrel.

Celebrate your home with a Stock the Pantry party!

Grow the Garden Party

This is one of my favorites as I've come relatively late to the realization of a green thumb. The Grow the Garden Party is ideal if you enjoy potting house plants or dream of a cutting garden, or perhaps harbor visions of growing your own herbs and vegetables. Invite your friends to an outdoor picnic and while you provide the food and drink, ask them to provide a plant or garden tool.

Of course you may want to suggest gift cards from local nurseries for those that are green-thumb challenged, and you'll want to specify full sunshine or shade for desired plants. The point is that you get a more eclectic mix and, when all are in bloom, they remind you of each guest and his or her personal contribution. You could even name each plant with tags after the person that provided it.

Celebrate your home and Mother Nature with a Grow the Garden Party!

Demolition Bash

Okay, you've made the decision to remodel and it is a big project. Kick it off in style with a Demolition Bash.

Celebrate Your Life!

Perhaps you are tearing out the kitchen or bath and making way for a major update or reconfiguration. In any case, it's gotta go. Be sure you time this with your contractor's schedule, and invite friends to bring a dish and do a camp-out in your newly emptied space.

(If you have handy, careful friends, you can actually invite them to assist with demolition, but be cautious in mixing a party atmosphere with hammers and other serious remodeling tools.)

It is always rewarding to enjoy even a day of the space unfinished before the work of putting it all together gets underway. Do be sure you have made all of your decisions at this stage and you don't open up the event to brainstorming. Too many opinions will only result in confusion and frustration.

Remodeling can be an exhausting and sometimes chaotic process, so celebrating at demolition can make it that much more tolerable. Be sure to plan the next bash to coincide with completion!

Celebrate your home with a Demolition Bash!

Paint Party

Personally, I can't think of anything I'd rather avoid than painting, but I can do it myself if necessary and without training. (Heck, I once sponge painted my whole house, since the contractor had reversed the paint colors in the final coat!). But I do have friends who not only enjoy painting but actually find it relaxing—imagine it!

So if you have one or two rooms to get done and would be willing to do the same for friends or family (turnabout is fair play in this), plan a painting party. You supply the paint, of course, but I'm betting you have friends with extra drop cloths, ladders, and even brushes that will be game to come and join you for an afternoon or a day of painting to be rewarded with pizza and beer or a cold-cut sandwich buffet and icy sodas.

This can save the cost of a contractor and actually make an otherwise mundane and potentially arduous task fun. Many hands make light work, so invite others to help.

Celebrate your home with friends who help you transform a room or two with a Paint Party!

Build the Deck Bash

I've got too many do-it-yourself friends, not to mention handy guys I know, that think decks are the be-all and end-all of projects. And there is a wealth of manuals on the market for just such a design dilemma. Now, if your deck will be more than just coming off the back of a house with a low drop-off (foot or two), you need to have someone who really knows their stuff on hand. Often you may not be building new but simply replacing existing decking with new boards or adding a new railing, both appropriate do-it-yourself tasks.

Celebrate Your Life!

You provide the lumber, food, and refreshments and invite friends in the know to bring tools, tunes, and a desire to work. What would have taken you a month of weekends can now be done much faster with the company of good friends, and it has turned into an experience rather than "the project that wouldn't end." Be sure you have a plan to either dispose of or donate the old lumber if replacing an existing deck.

Celebrate your home and the great outdoors with a Build the Deck Bash!

Deck the Walls Celebration

Got all your furniture in place but nothing to deck the walls? Make it an event and have guests bring you art for your home. Now, I know it is a little dicey to rely on someone else's taste, so you provide guidelines. You can also register and it doesn't have to be at some expensive gallery (though go for it if you can!). Consider art from national sources like Pier 1, Z Gallerie, and Crate&Barrel or online resource art.com. Many of the major retailers and catalogue companies have registries, and not just for brides anymore.

Alternatively, you can rely on just providing a color palette and style, such as Tuscan Countryside, Urban Sophisticate, Coastal Breeze, or Classic Traditional. This gives a bit more latitude and creativity to the gift giver. While you may not love it all, you will know that they gave it some thought and you can always pass it on

©2006 Melissa Galt

later. (I don't believe in saving gifts because of who gave them. I also don't ever check my friends' homes for the gifts I've given—goodness, I don't usually remember what I gave!)

Once everyone has arrived, be prepared with a hammer, tape measure, pencil, and picture hangars to literally hang it all on the spot. Or, hire an installer during the celebration to do this for you with guidance on placement. Everyone will want to see their treasured gift displayed (at least this one time) and know they made a beautiful difference in creating your home.

Celebrate your home with a Deck the Walls Celebration!

Dress the Bedroom Bash

Bedrooms are all about rest and romance. Keep the exercise equipment elsewhere and the desk for work in another room. I've also found that too often the bedroom is the last room decorated and often waits until after the great room, kitchen, kids' rooms, and bathrooms are done. Yikes! Your bedroom is your haven and deserves to be a priority. Don't wait; celebrate it with a Dress the Bedroom Bash.

It is up to you to furnish the bed—that means headboard, footboard optional, and a bedding scheme. The rest you can leave up to friends. They can provide actual furnishings in the form of night stands, lamps, pillows, window treatments, or a chair, or they can give gift certificates. On the invite, include a picture of you lounging on the bed, or your favorite Fido or Rover doing the same, and invite friends to fill in the gaps.

Yes, you can register for pieces if your friends are decorating-challenged or you just don't trust their taste! Most often you can make returns, and it may be fun to see what someone else has in mind with your bed style. You just might find yourself stepping out of the box and getting something more than you expected.

Celebrate your home and optimize your rest and romance opportunities with a Dress the Bedroom Bash!

Knick Knack Party

Perhaps you've gotten all your major furniture pieces in place and even have some artwork hung but lack the finishing touches that really make a house a home. So invite your friends to help provide the accessories!

Again, you can register for specific pieces like picture frames, candles, glass bottles and vases, wrought iron figures, florals and greenery, or you can trust your friends, with just a bit about your style in the invitation and a picture or two to give them a head start.

Of course, gift certificates do give anyone an easy out and ensure you get what you want. And you can always do an exchange later. The more information you provide the more likely you are to get tasteful elements that really add polish and flair.

Celebrate your home with a Knick Knack Party!

Spa Bath Moment

It seems every party I go to, someone brings the hostess a basket of bath goodies. This is usually much appreciated (except by those of us who are strictly shower types!) and is an easy way to get friends together to celebrate.

Plan a Spa Bath Moment that includes sharing your favorite scents and colors. Do you enjoy lavender or eucalyptus? Lemon or grapefruit? Are you into fruit or flowers, herbs or grasses? There are so many lotions, potions, aromas, potpourris, candles, and more to choose from.

You provide your preferences and consider bringing in a manicurist or masseuse for mini treatments for your friends. Yes, it is usually a girls' night only. But you can always expand it to guys being included if you have a handy project, like a tub to be replaced or just a new shower head installed.

Celebrate your home through relaxation and rejuvenation with a Spa Bath Moment!

Affirmations

I honor my heart by decorating my home with passion and creativity.

I enjoy the help of others on house projects that benefit from many hands.

I celebrate each new success and completion in my journey of creating my home.

My joy is multiplied by sharing the gifts of my home with others.

DIY tasks are a way for me to share with friends and family the creative process of my home.

Celebrate Your Seasons and Holidays

Seems we always wait for a holiday to celebrate and share time with friends and family. We don't often make time otherwise, and therefore I advocate creating your own holidays. At least turn some of those that seem to be just days on a calendar into something special and a way to connect.

Celebrating doesn't need to involve a lot of planning; it can be as spontaneous as calling friends in for a potluck supper, or even easier, getting a group together for pizza and a game of Trivial Pursuit. There are far too many opportunities missed and so much time spent focusing on the pursuits of career and job. Realize that all that we really have to hang onto are the experiences we create and the relationships we develop. Celebrate!

Here is just a handful of ideas to get you started on celebrating your seasons and holidays.

A Spring Garden Party

You could even call this a May Day Dance if you want. As kids we used to dance around the May pole at school. For adults the arrival of spring, more often than not, simply heralds the onset of allergies to spring pollen. Let's take time to think about the glorious greening going on around us, as all the plants and trees that have been dormant through the winter come into their own.

This is a perfect chance to enjoy the garden, get the spring flowers planted, and share an outdoor gathering with friends. Decorate with potted bulbs, tulips, daffodils, hyacinth, and iris. Make it festive with ladies in hats and gentlemen in bowties and bowlers (okay, if they insist, they can skip the ties!). Heck, maybe you can even talk them into seersucker for a taste of days gone by. Make it festive and an occasion.

You can serve that refreshing Southern tradition, mint juleps, and include chicken croquettes, mini beef Wellington, and shrimp and water chestnuts wrapped in bacon. Miniature pastries are a divine dessert. Dress up a bit to really usher in the new season.

Celebrate spring and the banishment of winter and cold temperatures with a Spring Garden Party!

Independence Day Fireworks

There is truly no better time for fireworks, though if it were up to me, they'd be part of every celebration! The ooohs and aaaahs at incredible shows of brilliantly colored sparks splashing across the sky and the low boom and high-pitched pop pop pop that accompanies just really lift my spirits. If you are truly going to enjoy fireworks, you need to consider whether you will create your own show (safety first) or head someplace to be in the stands. Yes, I know traffic will be dreadful and parking a fright, but look past those inconveniences to the spectacular show and, most of all, to the reason we celebrate anyway—independence.

This is an occasion that truly demands picnic fare like burgers and hotdogs and all the condiments to complement. Deviled eggs and potato salad are always expected. Add watermelon or fruit salad if you like. Have some fun with some festive foods, like the red, white, and blue Jell-O snacks or a cake alight with sparklers.

Remember, it is all about comradery and connection when we celebrate Independence Day with fireworks and picnics. Celebrate!

A Beachside Bash

Depending on where you live you can make this all about seafood, such as having a clambake up North, or you can make it favorite picnic foods. Just leave the sand on the beach, not in your bite!

Those of us that don't live at the beach or have a vacation home near one often only get a couple of trips a year, so make it a really special outing. Rather than relying on the fast food that abounds, or the overpriced seaside dives, bring your own and invite friends or another family or two.

Celebrate Your Life!

Be sure to bring plenty of beach blankets, umbrellas to protect against the sun, and sun block at all levels. Beach chairs and loungers are standard for added comfort, as is a good old-fashioned boom box unless you want to have an event with guests tuned in to their own iPods. (It would look like a bunch of disconnected zombies; there is no connecting going on unless everyone is hearing the same tune!)

If everyone carries their own goods and brings a dish, fun will be had by one and all. You can add sand castle contests, seashell hunts, sand crab searches, and pick-up beach volleyball. Relax, enjoy, and see what happens.

Celebrate the summer season with a Beachside Bash!

Lucky St. Patrick's, Get the Green Out

More than just green beer (never my favorite anyway!), this is about celebrating in March, midway between the winter doldrums and full on spring. It is also about being aware of the incredible luck and many blessings we all have. Too often we are tuned into what is not working and the misery in the world today (listening to the daily news fosters this) rather than realizing how truly fortunate we each are.

Well, clearly the theme here is easy—if it is green, it's in! So how many foods can you make green and still enjoy? Potato salad (or just do mixed greens), deviled eggs (or just do a mix of pickles and gherkins). Of course, you could also make it Irish and go with corned beef and cabbage, lamb stew and potatoes, or sausage coddle.

Share in the Irish tradition of the leprechauns and luck of the Irish with a celebration on Lucky St. Patrick's Day!

Memorial Day Grill Fest

This is the kick-off to the Summer Season and a valued chance to remember those that sacrificed their lives for our freedom and our values. Hang your American flag (yes, you can hang your state flag or another country flag beside it if you have one). Attend a parade; every small and large city has one. Then head for the backyard, park, or other venue, and fire up the grill.

Instead of the usual burgers and dogs, mix it up a bit and go for kebabs. You can do chicken with pineapple and peppers, beef with onions and tomatoes, and shrimp with sausage, mushrooms, and apricot marmalade. You can also do grilled vegetables on a stick, like squash, eggplant, and potato. Then if you keep the skewer theme or lunch-on-a-stick theme going, consider fruit on a stick with chocolate dipping sauce, or even pound cake and marshmallows on a stick with the same dipping sauce. Get creative!

Celebrate Memorial Day with a Grill Fest all about food on a stick!

Celebrate Your Life!

An Autumn Picnic and Hike

Watch the seasons change, stroll amongst the falling leaves, jump in a leaf pile, and sense the crispness in the air. Plan an autumn picnic and hike. Hike doesn't mean more than athletic shoes without a heavy backpack required—this is just a day trip. Have everyone pack their favorite sandwich, home-baked cookies, some chips, and a favorite fruit. Head down a trail to explore a sunset lookout, a breathtaking waterfall, or a panoramic vista from a rock outcropping.

It can be more of an adventure walk than true hike, if that is more appealing. Be sure to stop and check out the beauty of nature along the way. Explore unknown flora and fauna. Take your pocket guide with you to identify new finds. Breathe deeply in the fresh air. There is no real destination, so skip the agenda and just meander (well, don't get lost!). Be sure to take bug repellent and sun block if needed. Take plenty of water and be aware of your surroundings.

Find your perfect picnic place and take a break to enjoy the peace and quiet of the environment. Listen to bird songs, the crunch of the leaves under your feet, the wind through the trees and grasses. If there is a burbling creek or swirling river somewhere nearby, it adds another dimension. Leave the iPods at home and listen to the song of nature.

Celebrate the change of the season with an Autumn Picnic and Hike!

Celebrate Your Life!

Labor Day Cookout

Yes, this is the celebration of workers and we all are workers in some regard, so it celebrates each of us and our contribution! This also often heralds kids going back to school in much of the country. Make it a memorable last hurrah until your next holiday (or your Autumn Picnic and Hike).

Plan a relaxed bring-your-own event with friends and/or family. Make it a barbeque event with corn on the cob, burgers and hot dogs, chicken, macaroni salad, marinated green beans, cupcakes, and cookies. Don't do it all yourself; bring-your-own means more than just something to drink. Make sure it is paper plates and plastic cups for easy cleanup, and do your part by recycling. Celebrating those that built and continue to build this great country without protecting and preserving our environment is a bit of a conflict. Let's take care of what has been handed to us.

Celebrate the contribution of every working man and woman with a Labor Day Cookout!

Happy Birthday to Me

I'm not one to run and hide from birthdays no matter how many years pass. I firmly believe it is a celebration of accumulated wisdom beyond years and deserves a landmark every 12 months! I also believe that unless you have family or friends that make it the event you want, it

Celebrate Your Life!

is up to you to make it special. So I always plan a birthday bash!

Now, I am an advocate of catering or potluck so the birthday person isn't left with all the preparation. Get some friends to help with decorations and either ask one to serve as bartender or hire it out. There are also service companies you can call that will provide servers, and the same folks clean up. (There is nothing more unappealing than an awesome party followed by staying up half the night to clean up or coming down the following morning to a mess.)

I've also learned to make this a give-back occasion. None of us truly needs more stuff in this day and age, so I pick a favorite charity: consider Goodwill, The Ruby Slipper Project (helps victims of crisis and disaster reestablish their homes), Hannah Home (aids battered women), Salvation Army, or any cause dear to you. Be sure to note on the invitation that donations are requested to this charity in lieu of gifts. Donations can be brought to the party and then delivered in sum. It becomes a real feel-good event for all invited.

I also use parties to expand my circle of friends and always include two or three new friends so they can make their own connections and, in turn, extend their circle of influence. Life is in the relating and I want to forward that. It is always an eclectic mix, not one of those where everyone knows everyone and works in the same place—mix it up. It can get to feel like a day at the

© 2006 Melissa Galt

office if you don't include that quirky distant cousin or your neighbors.

Celebrate your years of wisdom with your own Happy Birthday Bash!

A Marshmallow Fireside Roast

S'mores are not the kits you purchase at the grocery store but instead are the good old-fashioned combination of Hershey chocolate bars, graham crackers, and toasted marshmallows. I can eat barely two without feeling a complete sugar-rush, but it is a whole experience and less about the eating than about the fire and the friends and family.

This is far and away best if it is an outdoor fire— bonfire scale is outstanding, but a chimenea or open pit will do. There is also something more fun about a marshmallow on a sturdy stick instead of on a metal skewer. Besides they tend to stick better to the stick than the skewer, and it is always a bit tragic to see your best marshmallow slide off unexpectedly to be devoured by the flames instead of landing between the chocolate bits and in your mouth.

I've been known to include sparklers at an event of this nature, to write your name in the dark, of course. I also encourage a beverage of choice, perhaps hot chocolate or, if of age, a hot rum toddy. Remember this is winter fun, and a moment of decadence few of us indulge in, bringing back camping memories or childhood holidays in front of the fire. Ghost stories are expected.

Celebrate the cold weather and bundling up with a Marshmallow Fireside Roast!

Winterfest to Beat the Blues

This is the celebration to have between Labor Day and Thanksgiving, or you can make it between New Year's and St. Patrick's Day, or both! Often the time after the holidays and before spring can be toughest. Once the holiday decorations come down (regardless of what holiday you celebrate) and those gift bills arrive, and the cold and damp really set in, it can be hard to keep your spirits up. This a great way to beat the midwinter blues.

Dress the table in reds, golds, oranges, and all the warm colors to fight that seasonal chill. (Yes, even on the West Coast!) Resurrect some of your holiday favorites but with a twist. Consider a roast chicken instead of turkey (this is an easy ready-made purchase at most grocery deli counters) or a leg of lamb. Go for lumpy mashed potatoes and skip the gravy (everyone is probably on their pre-holiday or post-holiday diet anyway!). Do up some green beans with almonds, or maybe succotash; butternut squash with brown sugar and butter is a delicious warm up. If you provide the main course, let everyone else pitch in and bring an appetizer, salad, or dessert. No one likes to show up empty-handed and this makes it easy.

Celebrate Your Life!

If you've got a fireplace, be sure to have it stoked and roaring. Put on some favorite lively music to bring the beat up. And serve mulled cider or a full-bodied red wine to complement the food (yes, I know it is chicken and that would be a white, but make your own rules and just have fun).

Celebrate to beat the blues with a Winterfest!

Affirmations

I create my own special occasions to celebrate with friends and family.

Every season brings a new reason to be grateful and celebrate.

I honor the reason for our holidays and celebrate the gifts of those that have gone before.

I make entertaining easy and fun by including my friends and family in the planning and preparation.

Life is short, so I celebrate for every reason and no reason at all!

Celebrate Your Life Contributions

Many of us are caught in an endless loop of striving and never seem to arrive. For each goal we achieve, we don't take a moment to celebrate but just move right to the next one. No wonder we are burned out, overloaded, and stressed. This is about taking the time to truly celebrate your life achievements and contributions— everyone has them! This is not just about ancestors, although they do count. It is about the legacy that we are leaving and that has been left to us.

Here are some fun and different ways you can celebrate your life legacy.

Life Video

Yes, you can have a "This Is Your Life" video created! Certainly you could do this yourself using video and still shots incorporated with audio and music, but there are professionals that can do this for you. Personally I'm not a great editor and I would hire a professional editor in this process. While we may think only of doing this type of video for a parent, spouse, sibling, relative, friend, or work associate, why not count ourselves? After all, our own lives are well worth a celebration. This is the stuff that roasts are made of!

The video represents a compilation of your triumphs and successes as well as a few of the more colorful challenges (now at a distance, so you can smile about them). Highlights could include graduations, weddings, children, professional achievements, service awards, birthday milestones, trips taken, and more. It really is a special opportunity to celebrate your legacy or that of another if you are creating this for someone else.

Celebrate your life achievements with a Life Video!

Family Tree

Genealogy is so popular today. We all seem to want to know where we came from and who our ancestors were. Perhaps you are lucky enough to have a family archivist, but if not, having a chart done can be as simple as going online.

The fun part is determining what format to put this in, and one of the most effective I've seen is when a tree is literally painted on the wall (or on canvas and then framed) and the family members are written on the branches. It is both a decorative and meaningful family history. Photos can be included of each member as available.

Celebrate Your Life!

This project can take something that might be perceived as a dry report and make it a tangible, easy-to-understand, and fascinating learning tool about your family. Keep in mind this may or may not be something for display in a public area of your home. It might instead be just for family on an upstairs hallway wall or in a private study. The choice is yours.

Celebrate your legacy with a creative family tree presentation!

Suitcases and Symbols

This idea came from the landmark "Paperclip" project, initiated by school children in Tennessee to understand the Holocaust. They wanted to collect a paperclip for every victim; this became much larger than that and in fact is now a dedicated monument. In soliciting paperclips for their project from celebrities, politicians, and survivors alike, they got some unexpected windfalls. A handful of survivors sent them original suitcases from the time filled with photos and mementos of those that were interred, far more meaningful than just a paperclip. These suitcases told the stories and experiences of those that were lost.

Turning this into a contemporary project celebrating life and legacy, you could use one of your grandparent's old suitcases, if available, or pick one up at a thrift store. Collage the suitcase with family letters, photos, and other mementos until it becomes a piece of family history and a sculpture to be displayed. Often homes have a ledge over the front door in need of a family treasure, or there is room in a bookcase if you remove a shelf. Making family history tangible adds a new dimension.

Celebrate your family legacy with a one-of-a-kind suitcase of family history!

An Architectural History

Many of us have pictures of family at their homes, and often these go back decades and even centuries. An intriguing way to celebrate your family is to create a timeline either on paper or directly on a wall (how brave are you, coloring on the wall?) and add the pictures of homes or families in front of their homes as far back as you can. It provides a lively look at the changes in architecture and home design as well as a peek into the location and character of each dwelling.

This would be particularly effective in a long hallway or above a double doorway. Those with an artistic touch can do more than just a magic marker creation and can involve the kids with adding trees and landscaping and even cars along the way, again either on a long piece of paper or canvas or directly on the wall (if you move or want a change, you can repaint). Whether collaged with magazine photos mixed with historic images, or artistically rendered for a more elegant presentation, the choice is yours.

Celebrate Your Life!

Celebrate your family architectural heritage and legacy with a home line!

The Family Archive

Many families are lucky enough to have a self-appointed family historian. This person is great at keeping up with all the family photos, awards, events, births, deaths, and general family history. While it can be a lot of work, it can also be as simple in this technological age as asking each family member for copies of old photos (scanned for emailing is usually fine) and for any letters or clippings saved (copies are also possible for these elements). It also means requesting only the most important or interesting mementos that they may be willing to share or pictures of the same. Many people tend to hoard keepsakes, particularly of children until they grow up and the parents realize the children aren't interested in the collection.

(My mother got smart and at the time she passed, when I was 24, she had saved only a file folder about and for each of us with cards and letters sent and possibly one or two school art projects. None of us wanted more; that was enough of our childhood.)

Keepsakes can be compiled in a scrapbook, a specialized industry of its own today, or even maintained in active files, computerized for easy access or hard copied for tangibility. Sources such as the online and catalogue resource Exposures provide conservation page books just for archiving. You can add text in the margins or even your own speech bubbles, much like a modern day comic book. The key in scrapbooking is to make this an animated version of family history that will truly be an engaging and meaningful way to find out about the past. This can be a view that includes the triumphs and the pitfalls, individual achievement as well as family ties.

Celebrate your legacy with the creation of an ongoing family archive, whether a scrapbook or simply active files for lending and sharing!

Recorded for Posterity

There is a national radio program that showcases snippets of audio files entitled "This I believe." It is audio of all manner of people stating their deepest-held beliefs and is wonderfully interesting to listen to. NPR supports StoryCorps which is traveling across the country and recording ordinary people's reaction to their significant life events. There are also now audio histories of many famous figures available.

You don't have to be famous to create an audio history of your life and family. This can begin with taping the stories that great-grandparents shared and then grandparents passed on and so on. It always makes a difference to get the story from the original source rather than the embellished version that appears generations later. It is also true that truth is stranger than any fiction, so by recording these truths, you are learning more than you possibly could through just reading a book. Vocal intonation and nuances in delivery truly bring these stories to life.

It is the wisdom and experiences of the ages that is the gift in an audio recording of our elders. I so wish I had tapes of the stories my mother shared. I remember only that she was a gifted storyteller and the tales were colorful and fun, but few of the details remain.

Celebrate your legacy and family contributions by capturing stories on audio!

Photo Collage

This is one of the easiest ways to narrate and celebrate your family life. Now family doesn't have to mean siblings, spouse, and parents; it can mean friends you are close to and have chosen as your family. Photo collages can take many forms.

Sometimes this can be as simple as a large bulletin board with photos tacked up in an ever-evolving collage. It could mean using a series of black and white photos in either silver or black frames in a display on your stairway wall. It can be fun to do this with the antique photos of ancestors and elegant framing.

Also effective is using frames with multiple openings and assigning a theme for each set such as family, travel and adventure, parties enjoyed, kids' events, and such. These

Celebrate Your Life!

photo collages can be most enjoyed on stairwells, in hallways, or on a kitchen wall. You generally don't want to do this in a powder room—no one will come out!

The advantage with this over a scrapbook or archive is that this is enjoyed each and every day, and if you get the type of frames that allow you to change out photos, you can keep this evolving and changing as quickly as life does.

Celebrate your life contributions with a photo collage!

Write Your Tale

How many times has someone said, after we've shared a particularly entertaining story, "You should write a book"? Well you can! In fact, there are services dedicated to helping you do just that. You don't even have to be a writer to achieve this, but you do need to be able to convey the highlights and low points in an outline manner and let someone else fill in the rest.

No, you probably aren't going to have a bestseller unless your family has celebrity status and you have something truly juicy to share with the general public. These books are essentially for distribution to family and close friends. But it can be a fun way to share stories in a consistent, readable format. You can certainly include photos and illustrations. In this day and age of print on demand, a volume can be completed for as little as $40 per book through a publisher, or you can do it yourself through a copy service such as Kinko's, complete with binding.

Celebrate Your Life!

Celebrate your life contributions by writing your family history and stories for now and the future!

Personal Capsule

Most people are familiar with time capsules, often buried in connection with historic buildings or as school projects to be dug up later so others can learn the story of those that went before them. Why not create your own personal family capsule?

It is a fun way to get the whole family involved, even beyond your immediate family, including grandparents, aunts and uncles, cousins, and more. Ask each person to put one element in the capsule with their picture and a note. The clever part is in deciding where to bury it so that it may be unearthed later by someone else or even future generations of family.

The capsule can be as big or small as you want. There are great online resources to help you with the details and the materials. It does need to be air and moisture tight and there are, of course, suggestions for what to include. There are also important considerations in the burying, including the need to call your local utilities for locators before digging up your backyard! Just think about the mystery and magic that a message in a bottle conjures up and you'll have the right idea. A time capsule is intended as a snapshot in time of you and yours.

Celebrate Your Life!

You can also make a time capsule to be opened several years later by another family member. For example, there are resources that provide capsules for baby memories or wedding mementos or even graduation remembrances that you may want to open a decade or more later for grins and giggles.

Celebrate your life contributions by creating and burying a family time capsule!

Name It

I am always surprised when I find out that a friend's relative is the name behind some highway, landmark, bridge, invention, or such. I went to college with Greg Penske, and it took years before I put it together about him and the Penske trucking company and racing organization! So, what has your family name, or that of a relative, become famous for?

I know you are thinking this is impossible, and it might be that there is none of that in your family, but check it out. You may be surprised. I've a friend that I only recently learned is related to Eleanor Roosevelt. Many of us have very colorful and inventive family histories—we just don't know enough about them, and some of us learned these but didn't remember or realize how significant the contribution was.

My mother used to tell us stories about my great grandfather, the American icon and architect Frank

Celebrate Your Life!

Lloyd Wright. As most children and especially teenagers do, I rolled my eyes and tuned out. I didn't realize he was a big deal until I attended design school in my late twenties. (When he showed up in my textbooks, I figured I might want to know more!)

What unique specimens does your family tree sport? Celebrate your family by finding out about the famous, infamous, legendary, and significant!

Affirmations

I celebrate my life and family contributions by knowing about my ancestors and their contributions.

I enjoy photography as a way to surround myself with family even when they are at a distance.

I don't regret what I haven't achieved but rather celebrate my accomplishments.

I create a living legacy for those who will follow me.

I contribute actively to the archive of my family.

Celebrate Your Life!

Acknowledgements

Deep appreciation to Dr. Shirley Garrett, author, speaker, and mentor. She provided invaluable guidance and recommendations at the last minute that really brought this book to life.

To my Tribe who heard me talk about this for a good long while before I actually put fingers to the keyboard (not as romantic as pen to paper, but accurate!). Thank you for being so willing and encouraging.

Greatest thanks to my incredible editor, Zuzana Urbanek, who was so willing to work at the eleventh hour with all changes, who formatted this in a style I love and hope my readers to do too, who improved my writing where it needed it, edited me when I ran on, and forced me to clarify when I got muddy.